Black

Black

Poems by

Andra Durham

© 2026 Andra Durham. All rights reserved.
This material may not be reproduced in any form, published,
reprinted, recorded, performed, broadcast,
rewritten or redistributed without
the explicit permission of Andra Durham.
All such actions are strictly prohibited by law.

Cover design by Shay Culligan
Cover image by Andra Durham
Author photo by Andra Durham

ISBN: 978-1-63980-814-4

Kelsay Books
502 South 1040 East, A-119
American Fork, Utah 84003
Kelsaybooks.com

To Delmaria

You are my first love.

Acknowledgments

Thank you, Lord, for allowing me to slander myself.

Contents

Introductory Note

Earth:

Noun

1: a purgatoric realm.

Festival

We found ourselves wrecked
As children,
Awaiting the descension of a plane.

Gilded desire,
Elephant ears
And his patience too

Cements us.

Devotion,
Pure as those choir girls on any God—gifted Sunday.

You are my Vegas carpet,
Rapt and hypnotic.

Pretty Baby

You just feel so much,

    Baby

You just hear too much.

    Baby—

You speak little and whisper much.

    Baby,

Give to my touch.

    Baby,

Let me cleanse your feet to make you sensitive
And respondent to my touch.

    Baby,

Let me into your veins.

Charlie,
Kill me to know sin.

Seppuku

There is no art to war.
The beguiled narcissist drives a screw to mind
Trephined
To believe idiosyncrasies.

  The American Dream:
  Asleep in day
  Dreams to fervor
  Night.

Children graved,
Open burial.
No future to unveil
Except the tragedy of the time.

  Blood and grey,
  It is too fast for me.

A mirror maze of ideologies
Warps truth:

  Consumer to substance
  Aye, no manna for me.

Death of understanding.

Belly

I wish to hide myself
Inside your belly
So, you can digest me.

I gently hum against
Your churn.

You are Budai;
Process and know me.

Hu

I am a child
With joy
Arush as Hokusai's imagination
And thoughts bright as Nash.

I crushed a ruby and ate it like candy.

I regress to ant
And mature in wisdom.

It is Basquiat
Apart from a friend and the genius
Made schizophrenic
To draw chess in sand, with hand,
On the beach.

Dharma breaks.

The Man Who Sold the World

One kiss is a thousand summers.

He is the cathedral's hush
And it's holy.

He is the portrait of every man.

He waxes
And wanes with the moon

And casts himself over me
As the greatest shadow.

He shivers me;
Heat introduced to frigidity
Shivers too.

I am the wick
Overcome by his fire;
He is the confessor
And with him
I am nude.

Barbie

Under the sun,
I became equal parts a fool
With its blinding light.

The dog bites,
The hyena laughs
And a blonde is the underdog.

If lemon is a fruit,
I shall be a scientist
As
I do not wish to be like Moses.

Scorpion

It enters the circuit
And fires
Like the shot heard 'round the world.

I saw kintsugi on the street,
Golden cracks in broken things.

She used to be a poet
But turned shy.

I seduced mystery,
And recollect
Many shameless days and nights:

Our heat,
Molten flowers
And that flickering light across the street.

Synapses.

Paprika

What stains the soul
And grains the mind?

An absurdist's departure from logic
Or
A seahorse in binary?

The cold of his hand
Brushed against mine.

A sobering collision
Calmed by sorrow.

She preferred bubblegum,
I had only longed for cold air.

Golconda (Magritte)

Who tore the net binding the oranges?

It liberated laughter so bright.

Verily,
You,
Suspended in bemusement
Like a trapeze artist—
Smirked.

The orange hue danced.

You placed a daisy on my foot
And I twirled it.

Such a noisy, optimistic fruit.

The Pale Sword

Voices raise in cathartic song.

The final note
Sighs
And a hush falls,

Bereft
And forlorn.

A god diminished
As a midnight nursery
And sun.

From the heights,
The dizzying crest.

Contrition

All pretense,
All pride,
All ego—a dross.

Last night I dreamt of you
And awoke early this morning to tears running down my face.

Thence,
Burdened by sin and shame.

So, I abase myself
For You

Lash
And thorn.

Man in the Attic

I drank bleach
To erase you.

It burned my throat
And the memory too.

Exorcise it—
Till the shadow no longer chases you.

I drank it in haste.

Color is most vivacious
This time of day.

Coppola

You do not touch orchids.

They will surely whither and weep.
It is
A blade to a beautiful wrist.

Rich,
The virgins
Dance
Atop the chaise
Unbridled by male gaze.

In the bathtub,
She disappears
Below the water
And prays.

Dolefully,
Another sunset
Stained
Red.

You do not touch orchids.

Charlie

His eyelashes played the piano
As he fluttered
In the valley of passion.

We could no longer
Separate ourselves from
Ourself.

He is holy
And black.

I love him greatest and least.

“Please weary me father to sleep.”

I love him greatest and least,
And tremble as we sleep.

Dear Husband

I wish to be a
Virgin
For you.

Then,
I could be yours,
Girlishly
And totally.

Inside My Seventh Self

Your soul is a masterpiece of emotion:

I see pink,
A harsh streak of red,
A soft Black line
And flakes of gold.

There was an orchid cradled by sapphiric hands
And I heard Mingus too.

Untamed

You were draped in a burgundy
Pashmina
Across the room.

I simply would not meet your eye
And circled you
As flirtation.

I drink you
Because you are tall, dark
And handsome.

You wish to damn me
But I can only gift you my
Sanity.

Tupac's Rose

Sometimes I hear the sea in the wind;

For a moment
Everything was caught
At orgasm.

Time suspends
Slowly
Then suddenly,
The world explodes

Like bourgeoning flowers in springtime.

Gemini

From a kaleidoscope
We see.

As Chaplain
We humor.

My heart is a tumult and it rages freely.

I am a butterfly of emotion;
Soft
And flitting.

I hold both joker high
And low

Though somehow,
I am under the earth.

Red

“Baby the devil is in my ear,”
I cried to my lover.

He responded,
“Baby, I hear him too.”

Lest We Forget

To be alive in such a poignantly ghetto time is . . .
Refreshing.

I need to take my wig off too.

Keep the Light Inside the House

I absorbed too
Little
And began seeking more . . .

And I became stained by the world.

Substance
Never spoke.

Depth sounded reminiscent
Of a Kardashian,
And oft repeated herself for profundity.

Time stutters;
The pain is incommunicable.

Ivory

The profane escapes me
Expressly
Its shock:

Purity is costly.

All the saints
Part with the world,
And here I am in
Vegas.

Where do nuns go before
They die?

Nora

You speak like moonlight
And dazzle like the Melissani at
Twilight.

Though you have scales
And a dangerous
Mien.

Your body is soft and feathery
As young men
Imagine a woman's body to be.

Though you throw
Tantrums
And oscillate like a pendulum.

You are good
And I hope this world remains good
For you.

Error

A mind deluded
Like watercolor with too much water.

Not hardware—
Nor software.

Each nerve surrenders to slow dissolution.

I curl inward.

Memory bleeds into memory
Until yesterday flows into
Morrow,
And I cannot tell which fantasies
Are mine and which belonged
To the rain that ceaselessly falls.

Vertebrae

You denied my love because
You feared forgetting your name
To mine.

You worshipped me.

Unfold me,
One crease at a time.

Devotion begets
Itself.

I will show you.

Love Is . . .

You slumber as I speak,
So, I quiet as the moon
To capture
Solace for thee.

I forgot how your voice sounds
At dusk,
Just before the sun.

A wave and
Sun
Curdle to mimic
Us.

Laughing and kissing you
Touches tender
My womb.

I've already said it.

Five Minutes

It does not matter who it is,
Did you experience God?

In the concert hall,
Do you hear?

On the beach—
Do you walk along the shore
Or tarry on gravel?

At dusk—
Do you sing?

I give you permission
To touch my soul.

I found Him here.

Phantom

Burnt lavender
Echoes
Like the stain of chalk
On black trousers.

Memory washes away
As chalk.

The mountain weathers but does not fold
Like a house of cards.

Permanence is illusion
Yet in collapse
I found Self;

We build castles the tide will claim.

The Wind in May

We plowed in the field of love,
Such glistened labor.

We sowed ecstasy
And pure delights.

The breeze,
Your sweet sigh
And hitch of breath, mine.

I could die in your embrace,
Baby,
Stretch my hands to the sky.

The Spook of the Angel

Furnaced,
Rotted wood
At your alter.

Black lungs
Groan:
Cylindric and limp.

To be the nail that pierces you
Slows rust.

Body to your wine
And sabbath for your holy.

Bauhaus

The cherry
To rot.

Table d'hôte
For a wolf
And black cactus for the flock of lambs.

An Akashic scroll
To Hitlers
Hands.

A brittle lament for erred

Order.

Giun

Fourscore years and one.
The sky
Plummets
And falls.

Water itself thirsty
Finds itself in the spring
Beside itself.

Yet I cannot tarry any longer.

I cast the pen aside—
From here I'll speak to the sun
Eye to eye.

Grief Aperture

I no longer trace your scent
In bedsheets
Spun.

Your pulse
Always hastened me.

I admit,
I had a swim
You were center.

Weary,
I stretched for you.

Drawn,
I sang for you
Hymns.

Lonely,
I bore myself.

Delmaria

Women turn to stone
Yonder
In the garden,
As envy hardened their hearts.

Basho gave depth
To haiku
Verily from you.

You are the geisha's moon,
The queen's crown
And art in motion.

The peacock mirrors your gait,
And the saxophone teases your age.

The Birds of Paradise rise for you—

Because you are sunshine,
Necessary and brilliant.

Stay Ugly

Stay ugly
Like rage before it learns to crack a smile,
Like grief before it is compartmentalized
And dressed in Sunday best.

Stay ugly
When they offer prettier words
To replace your angst,
When they suggest a softer way
To wear your skin.

Stay ugly
Like survival,
Like freedom,
Like power won.

S. Maharba

Do you collect secrets
As an eye and telescope
A cosmic sea?

My mouth runs like Niagara
Though I whisper
Like distant spheres
Amongst a universe of sound.

I long to hear the heaven song

Again,

A lyre,
Loot
And barefooted, drumming feet.

It was her who sang to me.

The Empress

I am opera:
Fear me or cower,
Whisper
Or cry out—
It is all the same.

I am the sovereign.

Kabuki for rage,
Lilies for despair
And shadows for longing.

I am diptych
And double,

A rare coin.

Closing Note

Karma:
Noun
1: to be black.

About the Author

Andra Durham is a multidisciplinary artist that advances critical cultural dialogue and demonstrates an unwavering commitment to amplifying essential messages in contemporary art. Through poetry, sound production, modeling, visual art, and event curation (Notsuoh), Durham slices through conventional artistic boundaries like obsidian through silk. Notable examples of work include participation in the Cave Canem Houston Regional workshop, "Further Invention," Fractured, *Yet Healing* (Wipf + Stock), and Free Improvisation (Nameless Sound and Volta MX) under the name "sanctuary." Durham's multidisciplinary practice need not ask permission to exist; and so, it further expands space for greater artifacts of truth.

www.ingramcontent.com/pod-product-compliance
Lightning Source LLC
LaVergne TN
LVHW050945080826
845145LV00004B/1419

* 9 7 8 1 6 3 9 8 0 8 1 4 4 *